Dirt-Cheap Prepping:

How to Prepare Everything You Need for a Disaster And Save Money

Table of Contents

Introduction

Welcome to Survival: Cheap or Free Ways to Stockpile for a Disaster, a D.I.Y. book designed to show you how to save money on how you stockpile and point you in the right directions. Prepping for survival is difficult in the first place and with most of the obvious items being expensive, prepping for survival can be an absolute nightmare for you and for your wallet. That's why we've made this book specifically around providing you with either cheap or free ways to stockpile for your disaster. Let's begin.

Chapter 1 – Dehydrated Food

One of the primary ways to cheaply stockpile food is to dehydrate and vacuum the food for later use. The way food rots has to do with the oxidation of food, which means that if you can lower the amount of oxygen a food has then you can store it for much longer periods of time. This is an often occurrence with pork, especially ground pork, as a clever way to preserve the food for longer periods of time is to place the food in the freezer. When you place food in a freezer, the bacteria simply can't live in that environment, which means it will last longer but that doesn't mean that it will be completely devoid of rot as the natural enzymes inside of the meat will slowly break down the food over time.

Since enzymes are a chemical reaction, there is no way to stop them from doing this but enzymes break food down much slower than bacteria. Most stores will have dried foods, such as dried beans and peas, which are far cheaper than their canned counterparts. These dried bags of food are already dehydrated, which is why you need to boil them for at least thirty minutes to a day. A good way to cheaply stockpile food is to compare the practice to the preservation of the older civilizations, which means salt. Salt absorbs water in most items, which is why a high sodium diet often leads to water retention in the body. However, the sodium traps the molecules inside of its bonds, so salted meat will last out on a counter far longer than a regular piece of meat.

Having said all this, we have three different methods for preserving food but the primary method of vacuum sealing food is kind of expensive. Vacuum sealers run anywhere from $30-$1000 and this makes no sense whatsoever in terms of pricing. All Vacuum sealers that are sold commercially follow three concepts: use plastic bags, suck the air out, and heat the bag shut. That being said, if you can't afford one of these machines then here are some cheap ways to seal up your food.

Water Pressure

Items

- A Large Pot of Water, the bigger the better

- A zip lock bag with the food you want to vacuum inside. You want the food to only take up half the bag or less.

Directions

1. Lower the bag into the water slowly until you have the bag zipper touching the top of the water.

2. Close the bag.

3. Lift the bag out.

The bag should be vacuumed now, but this didn't get all of the air out. There was bound to be some air in some corner pocket and there's likely to be a lot of air left in the food. However, if you need soupy materials, like powdered milk, to last far longer then this is the cheapest way to do so. If you don't mind going a little higher in price, you can make your own vacuum sealer.

Homemade Vacuum Sealer

Items

- Syringe. You want to get one of the big ones.

- A couple feet of Airline tubing, some extra in case of mistakes

- 2 No Return Check Valves

- Three-way Airline connector

- Closed Ziplock bag with the food you want to vacuum.

- Packaging or Gorilla Tape

- Toothpick

Directions

1. Cut some of the Airline tubing into three equal length pieces. 2-4 inches

2. Connect each piece to the Three-way Airline connector.

3. Connect the No Return Check Valve to the middle piece of the connector tubing. These connectors will be marked with "IN" on them, use that side.

4. Do the same with one of the other pieces of tubing and the other check valve, but this time you should connect the side that says "OUT".

5. Connect the syringe to the last piece of tubing.

6. Then, connect a larger piece of tubing to the opposite side of the syringe.

7. On this tubing, you will want to cut off part of the end so that it is pointed instead of directly round.

8. Then, take a zip lock bag and poke a hole in it to feed the tubing through.

9. Start pumping the syringe to see the bag becomes vacuumed.

10. Once the bags has been vacuumed, take a strip of tape and place it over the hole.

11. Press down on the tape as you slide the tubing out.

Now, how about preserving food in the manner of salt? That is relatively easy and it needed to be easy or else the individuals of the previous centuries would not have figured it out. They weren't the brightest people and often thought rotting food meant that the demons had infected it. Therefore, when salt meat preserved food for longer the salt was seen to be able to protect from demonic presences.

Salt Preservative

Ingredients

- The meat

- A container containing a 4-to-1 ratio of water to Pickling salt, or if you can float an egg in it

- A container that has a thick bottom layer of Pickling salt

- A VERY LARGE box of Pickling salt

Directions

1. Add a layer of meat to the container that has a bottom layer of salt.

2. Add more salt.

3. Mush around to remove air pockets.

4. Once you have it packed full with either meat or it's just full, you want to pour that container of salt water into the container of meat.

5. Push it down

6. Store it somewhere cool or cold

This will make the meat last a couple of months as the old civilizations would usually do this to protect large batches of meat that couldn't be consumed immediately, such as in the winter or because there was too much of the meat. You cannot completely preserve meat because of the fat in the meat. Once again, the fat has enzymes that will naturally breakdown over time. These are enzymes in your own body; that's how your body releases fat after death.

The last option of this process is to dehydrate your meat, or your material, because the oxidation will get to your food before anything else does. Likewise, you can't very well vacuum seal hot soup so we not only need to cover dehydration, but we also need to talk about how to take liquid items and turn them into powder. For right now, though, we're going to talk about how you can made your own dehydrator.

Homemade Dehydrator

Items

- Small Space Heater

- A 1' x 4' x 1'2" Cardboard Box

- Plastic sheets with holes in them

- A Few 1'x3' Drying Racks

- Some extra 1' long Cardboard pieces that can be made into triangular prisms

- Some Velcro

- Scissors

- Packing Tape, Screws, or some other type of securing material

Directions

1. You will want to cut a square on one of the 4' sides. You will be using this space to push heat through the box.

2. Stand the box up so that the square is on the bottom part of the table.

3. Then, take the other pieces of cardboard and make triangular prism out of them by bending it at each ¼ of the width of the cardboard so that the first bent cardboard will be in front of the last bent cardboard.

4. Secure these horizontally inside the box so that the racks can lay on them.

5. You can then make your own way of taking the velcro and applying it to one of the flaps on the box to make a door.

There you go, just point the small space heater towards the hole and you have a homemade dehydrator. This will cost the same amount it costs to buy a small dehydrating machine, but when you scale this up then it becomes cost effective. Just doubling its size could save you hundreds of dollars. Depending on how you modify this design, you could easily fit up to 10 racks within a small space. A 10-rack dehydrator will often cost you $200 or more.

The best part about most of these is the fact that you don't need power in order to still use them. In a survival situation, these materials would be the least likely to be grabbed by anyone but a survivalist.

Chapter 2 – Turn Liquid into Powder

Warning – You need a flat whole rack with this and tarp paper. Most of these instructions assume you are using the dehydrator we've laid out above.

Perhaps the most useful part about preserving food is knowing how to turn liquids into powder. In a survival situation, liquids go bad extremely fast if you don't store them in a refrigerator. However, this is not true if you can turn the liquid into a power, because most of the time you can do this and save your liquids from going made for days, weeks, and even months.

Powdered Cheese

- Ingredients

- Chopped Cheese

- Cornstarch (optional to prevent caking)

- Grinder

- Dehydrator

Directions

1. Place small patches of cheese on the drying, rack or drying racks, and let dry for up to three hours..

2. Flip the hard pieces of cheese.

3. Let dry for another couple of hours..

4. Grind the cheese. To prevent caking, you can add a little bit of cornstarch.

There you have it. That will make powdered cheese, which you can then place in a vacuum seal in order to prolong the life of the cheese for a year to even three years in some cases. When you take it out again, just add some water and mix it in with another food to get that cheesy goodness.

Powder Milk

Ingredients

- Milk

- Dehydrator

- Grinder

- Tarp Paper

- Clips

Directions

1. Pinch the corners of the tarp paper and hold them together with the clips. You should have a bowl at this point.

2. Place this on the rack.

3. Measure out 1 Cup or less of Milk

4. Pour this into each tarp paper you use. 1 Cup or less each. You can use up to 2 Cups if you have a commercial dehydrator.

5. Leave alone until the milk cakes and hardens into a material you can grind.

6. Grind it and Vacuum seal it if you don't plan to use it in the next to weeks.

Milk is the hardest liquid to come by in the survival situation. Therefore, having dehydrated milk that has been vacuum sealed, which will last a much longer time, is a great way to have milk in a time where milk is nowhere to be found.

The last method is something you can do for nearly any liquid, besides water, that you want to turn into a powder that you can vacuum seal. The reason why this seems so simple, and yet can be hard to believe, is that you cannot dehydrate water. You dehydrate water and you have nothing left. However, solids like milk and even broth are different because it is a liquid but it is also a liquid that's mostly filled with solids. This means that one can take the water out of it and what will be left is a solid chunk of all the chunks that made that particular liquid quite tasty. That is then something you can grind down and put into a vacuum-sealed bag for prolonged storage.

Fruits

While you can make dried fruits super easy by just baking them for a long period of time, what about if you want some fruit smoothies at the end. Since we can dry milk, we should be able to dry fruit smoothies and this is completely true. In fact, all you have to do is make a fruit smoothie, the way you like it, and then dehydrate it in the same fashion as the milk. This will allow you to keep large ready made quantities of this and all you need to bring it back to life is some water. It might not taste as good as the original, but then again if you're at the point where you can't buy anymore then being able to take a bag out of storage to make one doesn't seem like a bad idea.

Why You should Save A Bottle and Find a River

The number one thing that is sought after in a major disaster is the almighty water bottle, but with a little knowledge you don't have to walk through waves of people in order to get to the water or even get that water in the first place. You can build a device, right now, that will almost always take river water and make it safe to drink.

When taking unsafe water and making it safe, we need to keep in mind a couple of things. I will go ahead and make a graph so that you can see the problems along with their solutions.

Problem	Solution
Parasites	Boiling
Bacteria	Boiling
Gathering	Container

Now, there is a very specific type of container that you need to buy. You need to buy a Fireproof Container. The first affordable instinct that you would have is to go after, maybe, a metal coffee container but most of them are lined with an insulator to prevent people from scalding themselves. This means you need to find a different type of container.

Camping 101

You need a camping pot or kettle, a tube, and a container. You pour the water, in water ever amount, into the utensil that will be hanging over the fire. You connect the tube to that utensil to collect the steam and slowly pour that into the container. This is camping survival 101, which is that you need a way to collect fresh water from any type of water source and it needs to also not kill you. Steam is an evaporative gas, so unless there was an airborne virus near you the steam will be clean of any minerals, parasites, bacteria, and anything else that is potentially harmful. Provided you have immediate access to the river, this will give you water until the river dries up or you die from some other issue.

The Soldier's Way

Ingredients

- Dirty Water

- Soda Bottle or other bottle of similar design

- A medium bowl of small pieces of Charcoal that has been washed, you can make small pieces by crushing bigger pieces found in a local store.

- Clean Sand and Gravel

- Drill or something to poke holes into the bottle lid

- Tissues or clothing

Directions

1. Poke holes into bottle lid.

2. Put tissues into the top of the bottle, making sure the lid is blocked by tissue. This will act as a filter.

3. Add a little of the clean sand and gravel in the space of the tissue and pack it down tightly.

4. Add all of the charcoal in the same manner. Half your bottle or more should be made of this charcoal.

5. Add a little more sand and gravel.

6. Cover this with tissue much like you did with the filter.

7. Pour water in and wait for all the water to slowly (very slowly) filter through.

8. Once that is done, do it once more through the same filter.

9. Once that is done, leave it in the sun for a few hours so that the ultraviolet rays can kill anything that was left over.

This is a method employed by some individuals in the military as a way to filter through lots of water in a time of need. You can actually drink it after the first filter, but drinking it after the second and the sunbathing brings the risk down considerably. These ingredients, except for the water, don't go bad so you can stockpile these materials sky-high, get tons of filters ready beforehand, and purify your own water.

The Life Straw

The last part of this is a rather new (2005) invention that you can use immediately and it works very well. The Life Straw is an invention that was designed for the poorer nations and environments so that they could have access to clean water in some of the worst conditions possible. These devices are usually $11-$20 a piece and each piece will last for a few months to a year. One straw can produce 264.2 gallons of clean water and you can stockpile these like you can the soldier's way ingredients. However! There is a huge however, they will only last so long, which is why the previous to instructionals show you how to produce clean water without the need of such a device. Relying on this one tool as a crutch could lead to disastrous results, which is why we included the other ways to get fresh water in a survival situation. The first way, Camping 101, can be used in the middle of the ocean if those materials are ready for you. The ocean is filled with salt, an unholy amount of foreign bacteria, and a few drinks of the water straight from the ocean can potentially kill you. In these books, we prefer to ensure that you have more than one way to do something to prevent too much reliance occurring on one or more items.

If you feel the need to buy bottles of water in an emergency situation, be sure not to throw some of the bottles in the garbage as you will come to find out that these bottles can provide some use to you in the future. The Soldier's way requires a bottle while Camping 101 requires a container. These bottles will be very important for you if you need to stockpile on them in the future. Additionally, it's always a good idea to have a couple cases on hand as they don't cost very much and, when an emergency occurs, the prices for water tend to skyrocket until the government intervenes.

Chapter 3 – Cheaper Gardening

You can start a garden without really spending any more than you already do, provided that you buy vegetables and fruits. The reason why this is important is because these types of foods have seeds in them and you are fertilizers. Oh, I should have mentioned this will likely gross some individuals out if they're not used to using feces as fertilizer. That's right, the fertilizer that you use at the store, the fertilizer that most farmers use, and the fertilizer that comes out of you all share a common ingredient: poop.

The Bucket

What you will want to do is grab a small bucket and start pooping, and peeing, in it for a week. Poop and pee have separate elements in it that help plants grow and most of it contains the nutrients that our body didn't use or find useful. Ironically, most of the nutrients that our bodies don't use or find useful are nutrients that plants love. The size doesn't really matter that much, just that you collect it and there's a decent amount. Once you've got a good amount, put a pair of clippers over your nose and grab some dirt because you need to mix the dirt with the poop. You will want to do this a couple of times throughout the week until it looks like fertilizer.

The Seeds

The easiest part of this are the seeds you will need to grow in your garden, which can be retrieved from the food that you buy. Until the fruit has rotten and withered, the seeds will be perfectly fine. In fact, the fruit is the initial food of the seeds as they grow in the ground. The important part here is find the food that matches your lifestyle and the seasons they grow in. For instance, Oranges are popular in Florida because they can grow around the year while this is not always true of the beans and peas that are sold in the same aisle, as they need a warm environment to grow. The lifestyle is important because you might not want a cactus, which requires very little work but you also might not want a fruit or veggie that you have to continuously water all the time.

The Garden

While you may not be able to afford a solid garden plot, you can afford the Cardboard Garden. The cardboard garden does a few things for you that a normal plot does not. The first is that it protects your plants from a number of small insects that cannot burrow through things. You will undoubtedly deal with pests, but the great part of planting foods with seeds in them is the fact that the weaker plants will be devour and you will have strong and healthy plants. You don't have to put this type of garden in the ground if you don't want to and you shouldn't if you plan to have plants that don't require a lot of room.

There are special types of gardens called garden rooms where people have shelves of different plants that allow them to grow throughout the year with controlled conditions. You can set this up to because it is relatively cheap, but you don't have to set it up immediately if you can't. Most of the instructionals within this book are made in a way that you can scale them to your needs. Therefore, if you want a garden that is five times as big then all you need to do is work five times the amount and get a bigger box.

Chapter 4 – Cheap and Easier To Grab Food

Now that we've covered nearly everything that you can do that would remove your dependence on the commercially operated franchises, there are a few foods that you can only get with them that can be very good inside of an emergency.

Tea Leaves

Not the tea packets you see in the store, but the ingredients that they are made of. Sure, you can buy the tea in those packets at around $3.00 each, but easy and lazy isn't part of the title, it's cheap and free. We've suggested some great cheap and free alternatives already, but tea has, by far, the wide bulk to single cost range of any item here. A pound of tea ingredients is usually $10. Meanwhile, the bags they sell you are 1.2oz for $3.00. That's right, that's nearly ten times the amount for the bulk and they also count the packaging material in most packages. Tea has a wide range of health packages and many of the ingredients simply can't be found locally. To grow them requires even more dedication as most tea does not come from America and, therefore, requires the conditions in which they are grown. Therefore, the most economical way to get tea is to buy bulk bags of it and then use a tea kettle that has a metal filter. This will ensure that the tea ingredients do not mix with the inside of the pot and you get the benefits of the tea as you normally would.

What are the benefits though? Why would you want tea as part of your emergency stash? Do you want anti-fungal, anti-bacterial, and anti-inflammatory natural medicine? The ingredients found in items such as black tea and green tea have these as part of their natural makeup. This is because the plants in them have those medicinal properties, so when you drink their tea you are getting those benefits. What most individuals in more modern societies don't know is that you can apply them directly to wounds. Some of them, like clove tea, are anti-septic. We could make an entire book on tea itself and its benefits, but that is not the scope of this novelette.

Rice

Rice comes from the East, for the most part, which means that it has to be imported here or grown in specific conditions. Unless you go about setting those conditions, you will want to buy the rice from the store. Don't worry, rice is incredibly cheap, especially if you go to an Asian Market or some similar Asian Food-based marketplace. Online, you can even find rice that is a dollar a pound and this food is extremely good for you for survival, provided you avoid "Enriched" rice. Enriched is a marketing terms used to explain that the ingredients have gone through a process that stripped them of any possible nutritional value, but they know people buy something continuously if they don't know this so they put some extra stuff in at a very low price so they can say they enriched it.

So, why should you buy it? One cup of rice mixed with anything you want is usually enough to feed an entire family. Provided you cook it correctly, one cup of rice will make the equivalence of half of a large pot. Mix it with practically anything, like some meat and veggies and you have enough to feed a family of four for a couple of days. This rice was specifically farmed for its resilience to conditions provided it was drowned in water, which matches a lot of areas in Asia, and the long amount of time you can store it in some location. Oxygenated rise can last up to 5 years while Oxygen Free Rice can last up to 30 years. Rice is a storage superfood.

Wheat Grain Bulk

One of the top foods that you will see in a survival situation is bread and lots of it, but this is also something you should store. You want to try and get the actual grains. You will also want to make sure you suck the air out of what you don't use because that is the only way that wheat grains will last for longer periods of time, but if you vacuum seal them then they will last for 30 years and more. Yes, wheat grains are like rice due to the fact that they can be stored for so long.

These three ingredients are something you can't get at home, for the most part, and they will be crucial for long periods of survival. The last a long time, come with healthy benefits, and they are cheap in large quantities and if shopped for correctly.

Conclusion

Welcome to the end of this book. We have gone over many different cheap or free methods of stockpiling for a survivalist situation. As always, this is not a replacement for research but rather a very good step forward in navigating the world of surviving. Most of these are small projects that can be scaled up to different sizes so that you can gauge just how much of it you will need to produce the needed amount of food.

None of these instructions are guaranteed to replace the grocery market completely, but they do have the potential to. Just remember that even if you are not trying to survive, being a survivalist can save you a lot of money if you let it and will give you organic food for years to come. There will be disasters in the future but, for now, good luck and better surviving.

FREE Bonus Reminder

If you have not grabbed it yet, please go ahead and download your special bonus report
"Preppers Survival Guide. Proven Tactics For Armed Incounters!"

Simply Click the Button Below

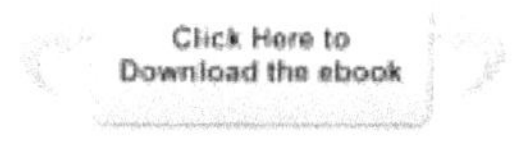

OR **Go to This Page**

http://preppersliving.com/free

BONUS #2: More Free & Discounted Books & Products

Do you want to receive more Free/Discounted Books or Products?

We have a mailing list where we send out our new Books or Products when they go free or with a discount on Amazon. Click on the link below to sign up for Free & Discount Book & Product Promotions.

=> Sign Up for Free & Discount Book & Product Promotions <=

OR Go to this URL

www.ingramcontent.com/pod-product-compliance
Lightning Source LLC
Chambersburg PA
CBHW061926270726
48659CB00002BA/980